BLACKS IN ANCIENT GREECE

by William S. Morison, Ph.D.
Assistant Professor of Classics,
Temple University

Drawings from the antiquities
by Nancy Conkle

We owe a great debt—as any work on this subject must—to the scholarship of Frank Snowden. For further reading, see his recent article "Greeks and Ethiopians," in *Greeks and Barbarians* (Bethesda, 1997), edited by J.E. Coleman and C.A. Walz.

The Greeks called the blacks who lived south of Egypt or south of the great Sahara desert Ethiopians, which means "burnt-faced men" in ancient Greek. They imagined that these Ethiopians lived close to where the sun rose and so had been darkened by its powerful rays. The epic poet Homer tells us that they lived at the edge of the world, along the streams of the great Ocean, and that the gods, especially Zeus and Poseidon, feasted with them often.

However, to the Greeks the Ethiopians were not only alive in myths. There were also black people who lived in the many city-states of the Greeks. Some had migrated from Africa to be merchants, others came as soldiers (some stayed, some did not), and some came as slaves. It is impossible to say how many black people lived in the Greek cities at any given time, but even the earliest historical and literary records indicate their presence.

Here is a young orator, a schoolboy from the Hellenistic period. He grips a scroll—maybe his homework—and concentrates on the day ahead.

From a bronze figure, c. 150 B.C.
Boston, Museum of Fine Arts.

From the Palace of Minos, c. 1500 B.C.
Herakleion Archaeological Museum

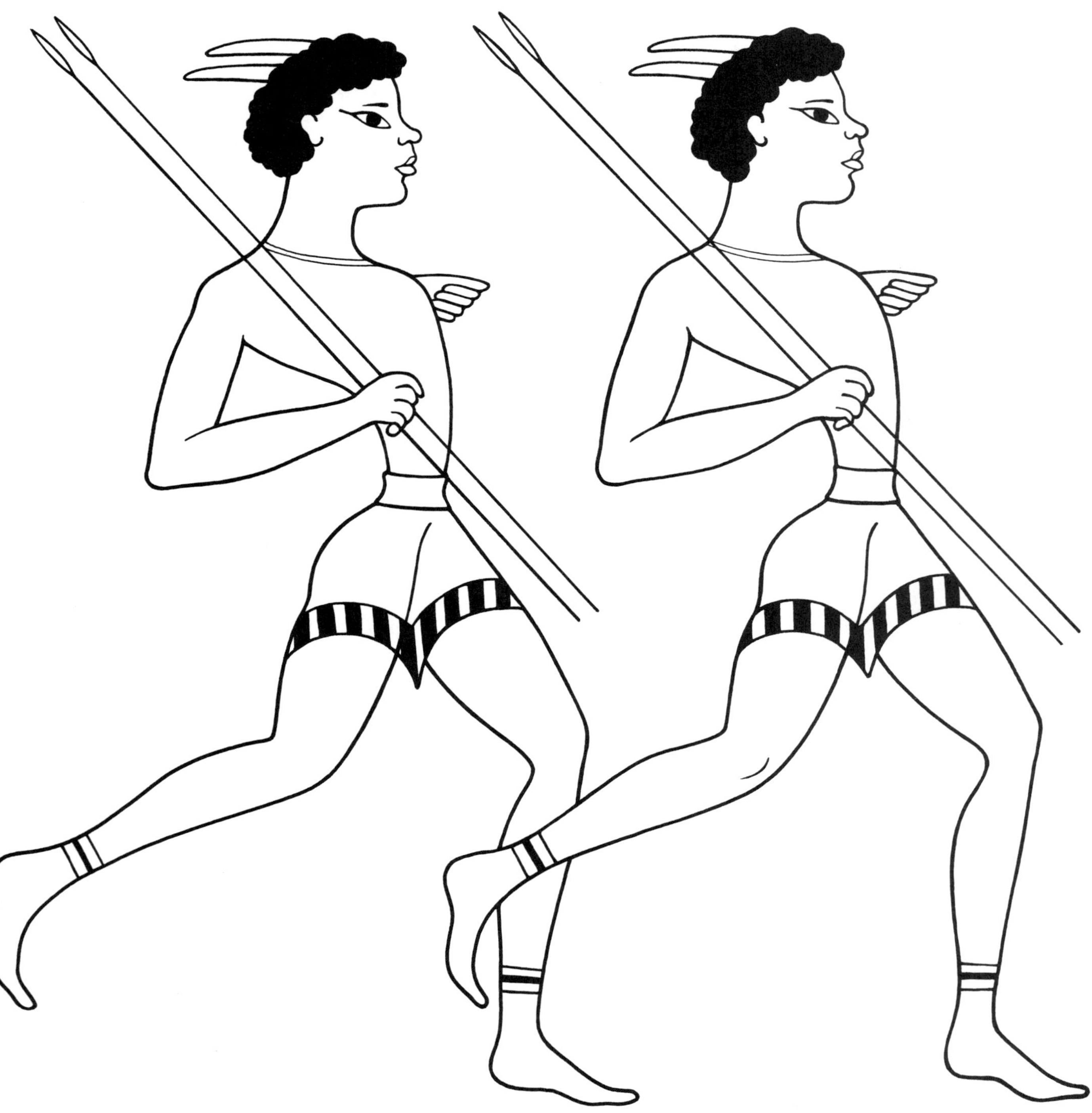

Archaeological discoveries at Knossos in Crete have uncovered pictures of black soldiers in the frescoes that adorned the walls of the palace of Minos. Here two soldiers wear the short kilts of Minoan soldiers and carry two spears each as they run forward. Other frescoes from the palace show blacks scattered among the general population of the city. The total number of black people that can be identified in these frescoes and in other Minoan art is significant. They clearly lived among the townspeople of Knossos, in addition to being soldiers.

On mainland Greece in the palace of Nestor at Pylos, a fresco dating to around 1250 B.C. shows a parade with both black and white males. Also found at Pylos was a list of property owners including someone called "ai-ti-jo-quo," which may have meant "Ethiopian."

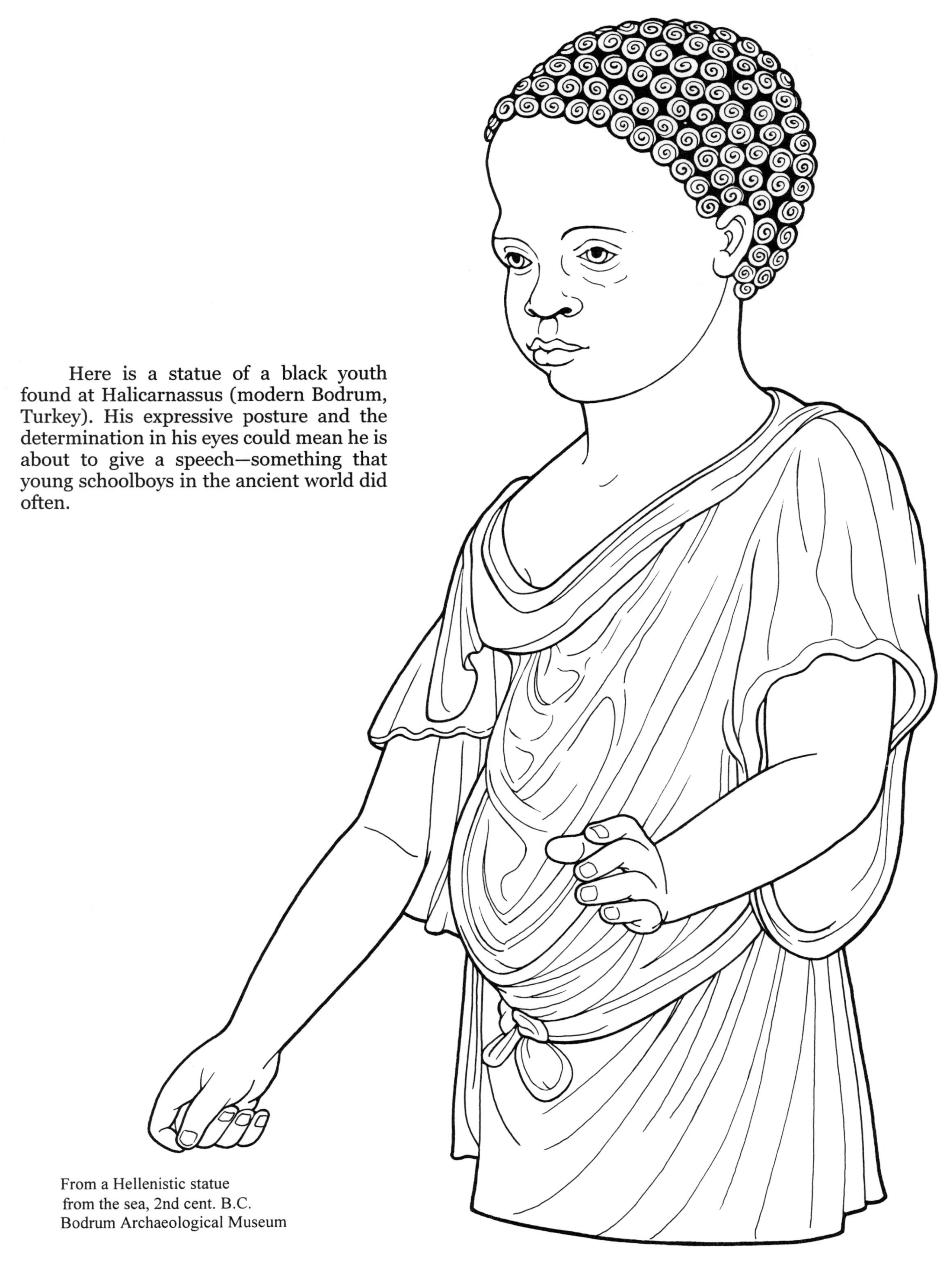

Here is a statue of a black youth found at Halicarnassus (modern Bodrum, Turkey). His expressive posture and the determination in his eyes could mean he is about to give a speech—something that young schoolboys in the ancient world did often.

From a Hellenistic statue
from the sea, 2nd cent. B.C.
Bodrum Archaeological Museum

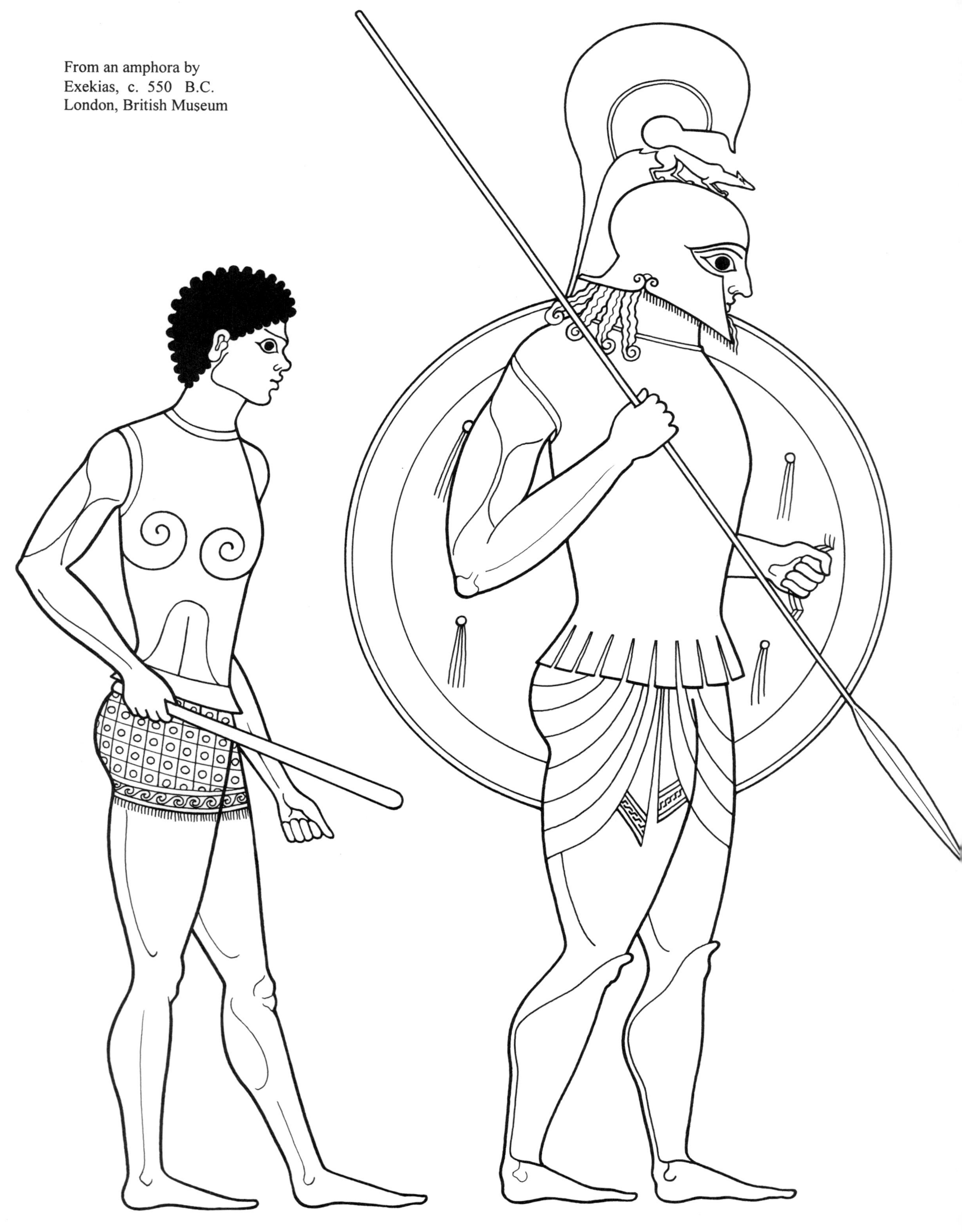

From an amphora by
Exekias, c. 550 B.C.
London, British Museum

Τιθωνῷ δ' Ἠὼς τέκε Μέμνονα χαλκοκορυστήν,
Αἰθιόπων βασιλῆα, καὶ Ἠμαθίωνα ἄνακτα.

Hesiod, *Theogony* 984-985

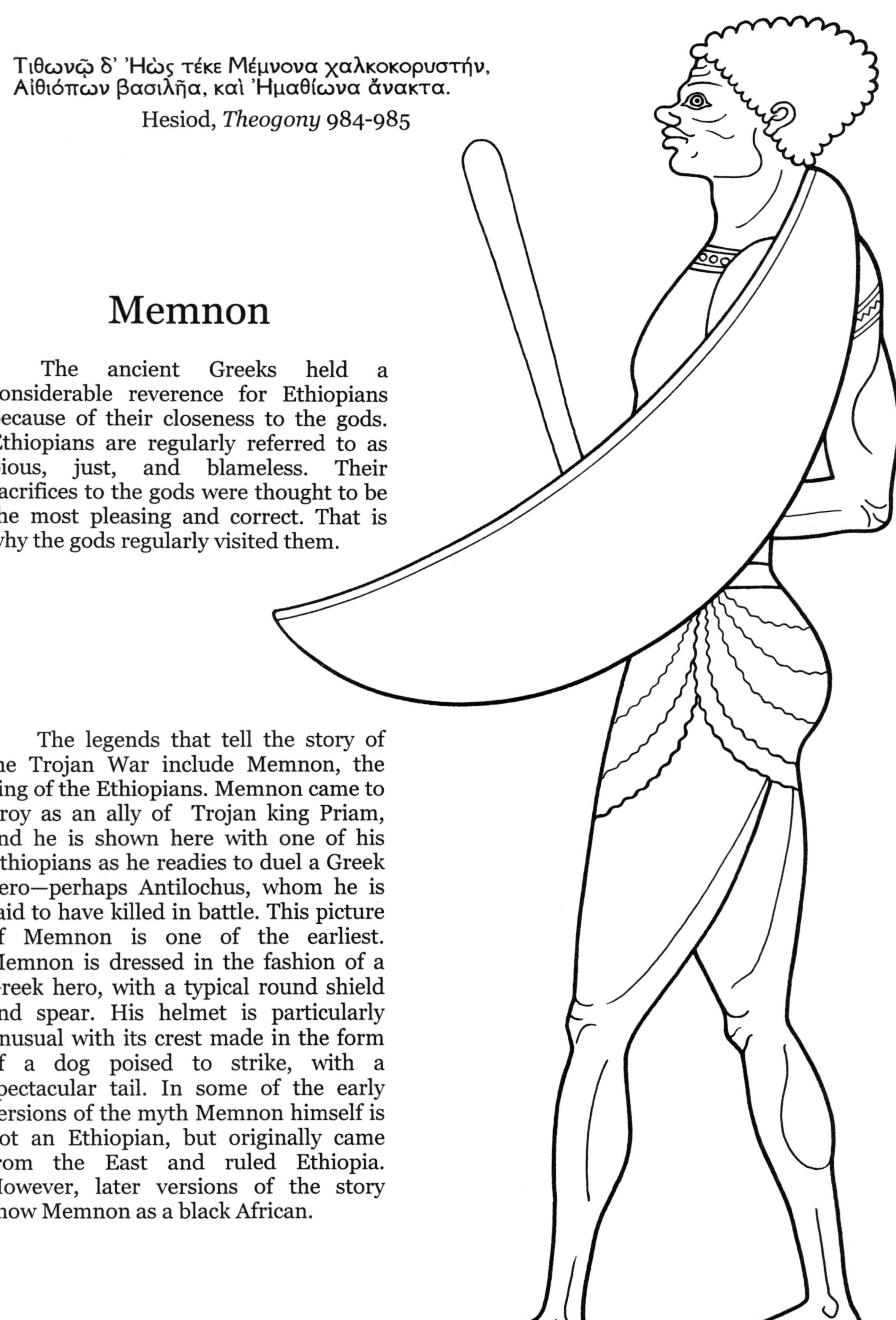

Memnon

The ancient Greeks held a considerable reverence for Ethiopians because of their closeness to the gods. Ethiopians are regularly referred to as pious, just, and blameless. Their sacrifices to the gods were thought to be the most pleasing and correct. That is why the gods regularly visited them.

The legends that tell the story of the Trojan War include Memnon, the king of the Ethiopians. Memnon came to Troy as an ally of Trojan king Priam, and he is shown here with one of his Ethiopians as he readies to duel a Greek hero—perhaps Antilochus, whom he is said to have killed in battle. This picture of Memnon is one of the earliest. Memnon is dressed in the fashion of a Greek hero, with a typical round shield and spear. His helmet is particularly unusual with its crest made in the form of a dog poised to strike, with a spectacular tail. In some of the early versions of the myth Memnon himself is not an Ethiopian, but originally came from the East and ruled Ethiopia. However, later versions of the story show Memnon as a black African.

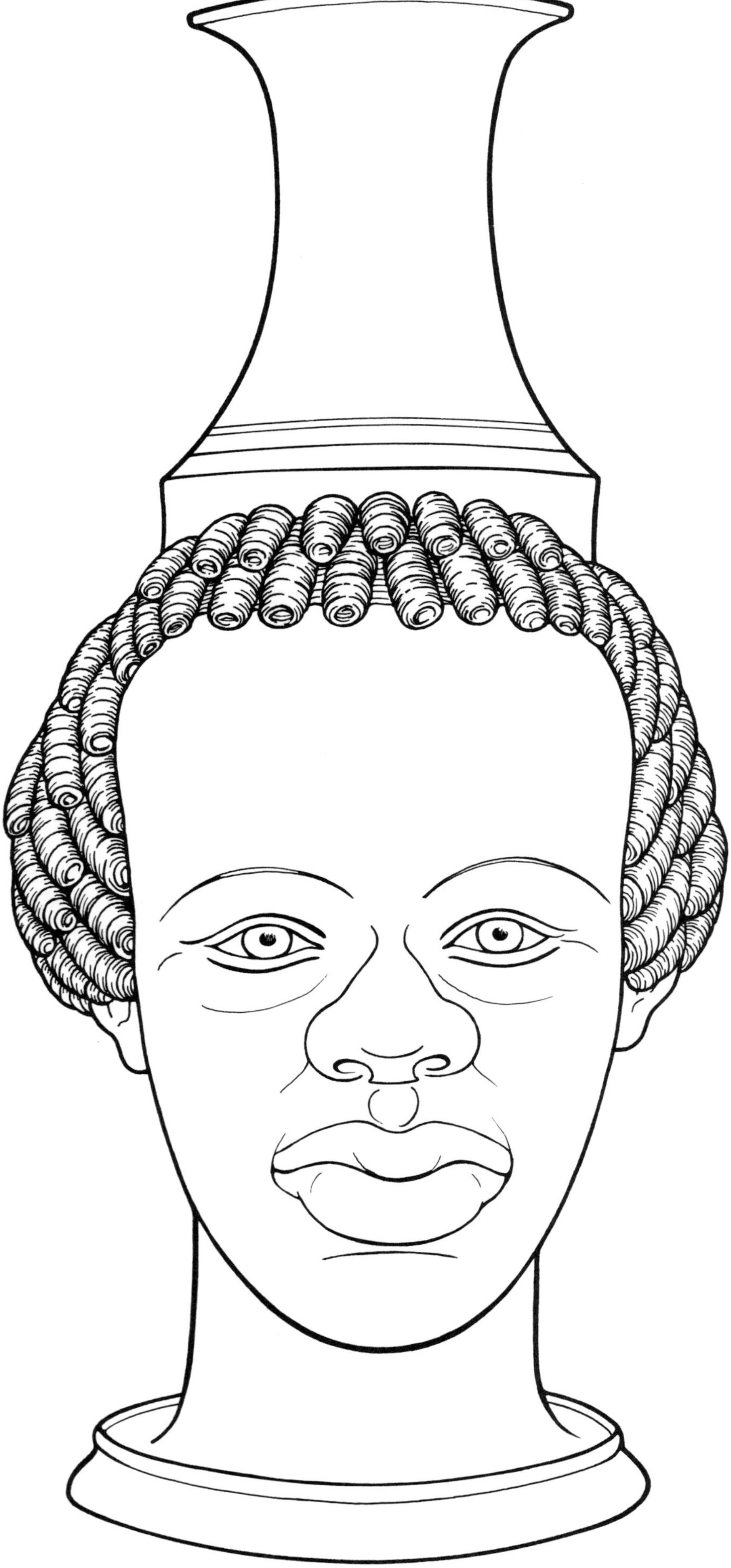

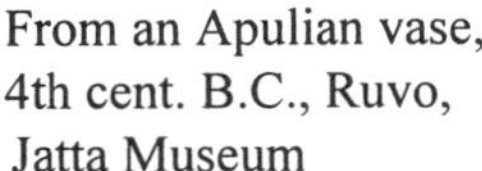

From an Apulian vase, 4th cent. B.C., Ruvo, Jatta Museum

Here is a beautiful vase in the shape of a black youth's head. The Greeks were fascinated by the physical differences among the various people that they encountered. Vases, pitchers, and drinking vessels shaped like the heads of black Africans tell us about this interest.

The Myth of Bousiris

During the reign of the Egyptian King Bousiris, who was the son of the sea god Poseidon, a terrible famine gripped the land. A seer named Phrasius from the island of Cyprus told Bousiris that in order to return fertility to the fields, Bousiris must sacrifice a foreigner to the god Zeus each year. Bousiris first sacrificed the seer and then, each year, another foreigner. Then, in the course of his many travels, the Greek hero Hercules visited Egypt. Here one of Bousiris' men has captured Hercules and is leading him to the king to be sacrificed.

Μετὰ Λιβύην δὲ Αἴγυπτον διεξῄει. ταύτης ἐβασίλευε Βούσιρις Ποσειδῶνος παῖς καὶ Λυσιανάσσης τῆς Ἐπάφου.

Apollodorus, *The Library* 2.4

From a pelike from Nola by the Ethiop Painter, 5th cent. B.C. Paris, *Bibliothèque Nationale*

Black Hercules

Αἴγυπτος προπάροιθεν ἐπ' ἐννέα κάρφετο ποίας   Callimachus, fr. 44

From a hydria from Caere, 6th cent. B.C. Vienna, *Kunsthistorisches Museum*

Here a black Hercules battles with Bousiris and his attendants. To the left is the altar, where he was to be sacrificed. The African location of this myth may have influenced the painter. Perhaps the painter himself or his potential customers were black.

Here Comes Help

Here a group of King Bousiris' men come rushing with curved sticks to aid their king against a rampaging Hercules...

Apollodorus, *The Library* 2.4:

οὗτος τοὺς ξένους ἔθυεν ἐπὶ βωμῷ Διὸς κατά τι λόγιον·
ἐννέα γὰρ ἔτη ἀφορία τὴν Αἴγυπτον κατέλαβε,

From the same vase
as the last pages.

Escape From Hercules

Other unarmed attendants, one with a pitcher and another with a lyre, flee Hercules.

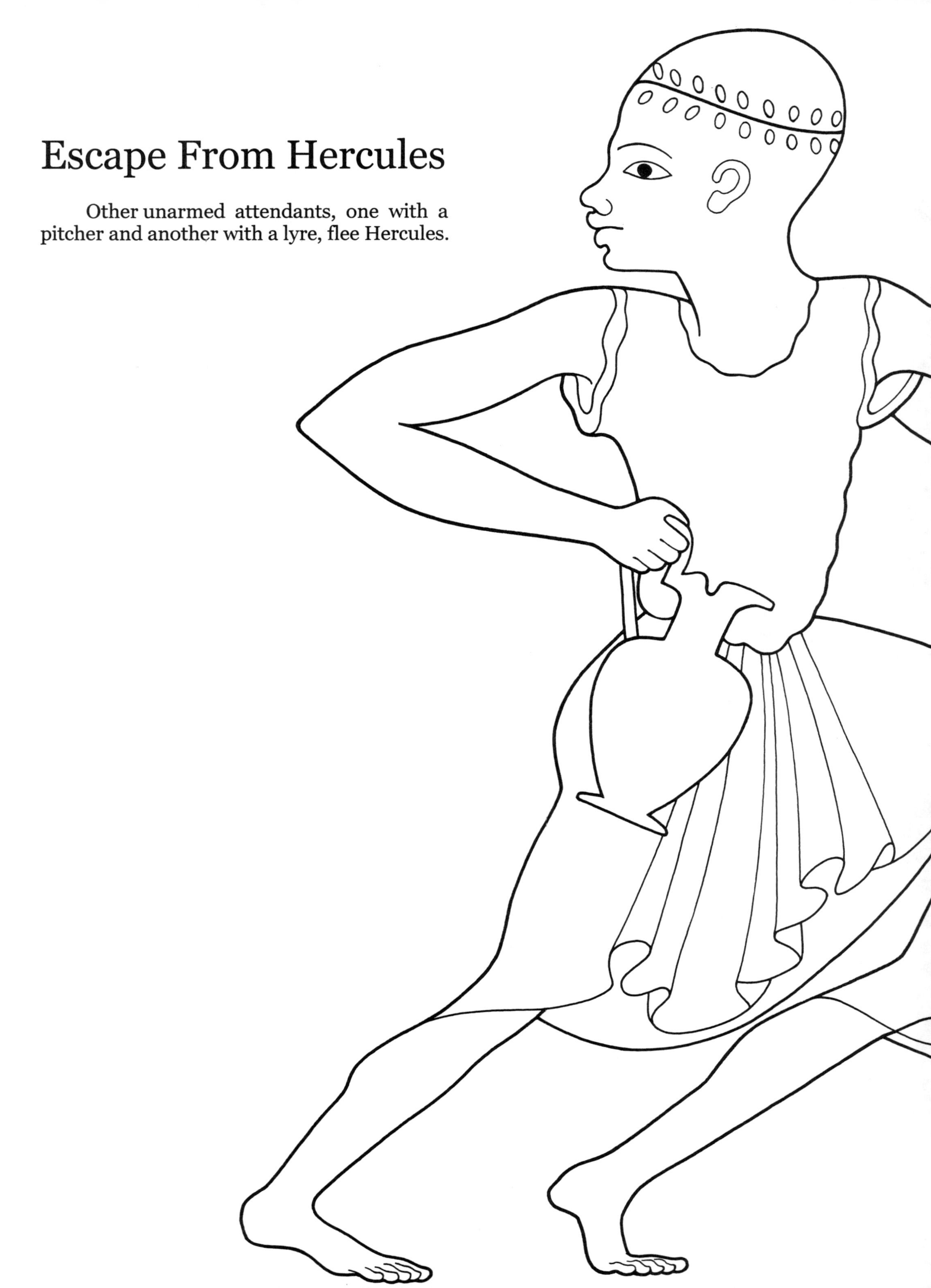

From a kylix by Epiktetos, c. 520 B.C.
London, British Museum

Φρασίος δὲ ἐλθὼν ἐκ Κύπρου, μάντις
τὴν ἐπιστήμην, ἔφη τὴν ἀφορίαν
παύσασθαι ἐὰν ξένον ἄνδρα τῷ Διὶ σφάξωσι κατ᾽ ἔτος.

Apollodorus, *The Library* 2.4

Here one of King Bousiris' men, paralyzed with fear by the enraged hero Hercules, is attempting to surrender.

From a pelike by the Pan Painter, c. 470 B.C., Athens, National Museum

Βούσιρις δὲ ἐκεῖνον πρῶτον σφάξας τὸν μάντιν τοὺς κατιόντας ξένους ἔσφαζε.

Apollodorus, *The Library* 2.4

Here another of King Bousiris' men
runs off with a pitcher of wine.

From a kylix from Spina, 5th cent. B.C., Ferrera, *Museo Archaeologico*

Apollodorus, *The Library* 2.4:

συλληφθεὶς οὖν καὶ Ἡρακλῆς τοῖς βωμοῖς προσεφέρετο τά δὲ δεσμὰ διαρρήξας τόν τε Βούσιριν καὶ τὸν ἐκείνου παῖδα Ἀμφιδάμαντα ἀπέκτεινε.

A Nike and Black Hercules

Hesiod, *Theogony* 383-384:

Στὺξ δ' ἔτεκ' Ὠκεανοῦ θυγάτηρ Πάλλαντι μιγεῖσα
Ζῆλον καὶ Νίκην καλλίσφυρον ἐν μεγάροισιν,

From a hydria by the
Nikias Painter, c. 400 B.C.
Paris, *Musée du Louvre*

Nike, the goddess of victory—not of shoes—and Black Hercules ride a chariot drawn by centaurs, who were half horse, half man. Hercules carries his club and wears his lion skin. Nike, whose name means victory in Greek, has wings, which symbolize how success can always fly away.

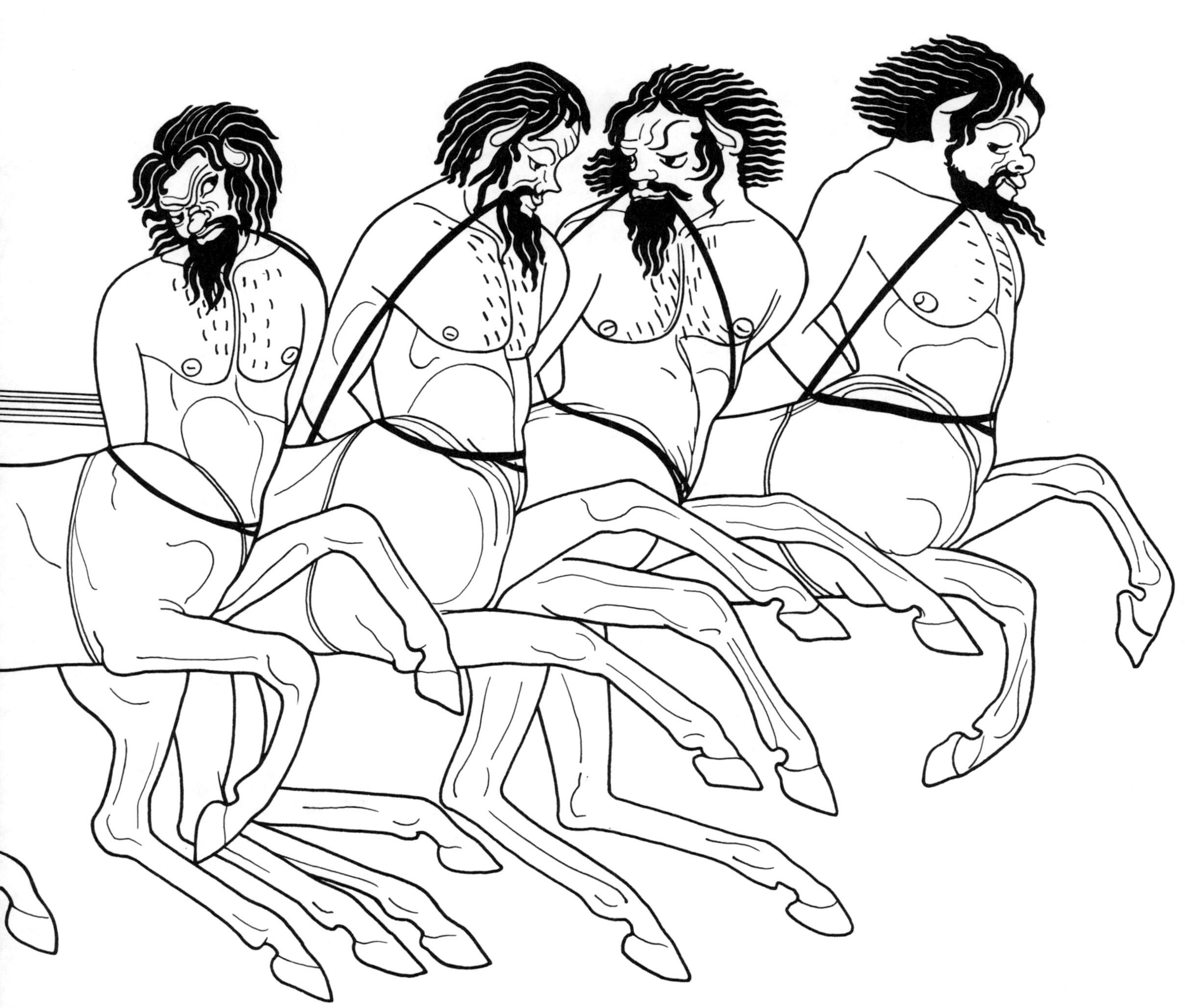

αὕτη δὲ ἐβασίλευεν Ἀμαζόνων, αἳ κατῴκουν περὶ τὸν Θερμώδοντα ποτάμον, ἔθνος μέγα τὰ κατὰ πόλεμον.

Apollodorus, *The Library* 2.5.9

From a wine jar by Polygnotos, c. 450 B.C. London, British Museum

Penthesilea, A Black Amazon

The Amazons were a mythical race of female warriors who are usually said to have come from the northeastern part of Asia Minor and northern Greece. The most famous were those who came to Troy to fight as allies with the brave Trojans against the Greeks, under the command of their fierce queen Penthesilea.*

*See Bellerophon's *Amazons.* There has always been a tradition of Black Amazons. Even before Cortez reached Old California (Baja Cal.), the story was told of that land's occupation by Black Amazons who raised flying griffons. Whenever little boys were born, the griffons were sent to drop them from the sky. See Bellerophon's *Early California,* vol. 1.

Here a Greek warrior moves forward with his sword drawn; he carries a shield with an Ethiopian herald holding a trumpet in his right hand and preparing to sound it. One of Odysseus' heralds, Eurybates, was black, and there may have been many others.

From a vase by the Kleophrades Painter, c. 480 B.C., Würzburg University Museum

From an amphora from Cerretri, 5th cent. B.C., Vienna, *Kunsthistorisches Museum*

Here another Greek warrior stands with his spear and a similar shield with a black herald sounding his trumpet. Again, the close associations that Ethiopians had with the gods in Greek mythology made them powerful symbols.

Andromeda

From a vase of the 4th cent. B.C.
Oxford, Ashmolean Museum

Andromeda was the daughter of King Cepheus and the vain Queen Cassiopeia, who bragged that both she and Andromeda were more beautiful than the sea nymphs, the Nereids. The angry Nereids complained to the great sea god Poseidon, who in turn sent a flood and a terrible sea monster to ravage Cepheus's lands. The oracle of Zeus told the King at Ammon that the only way to appease the god was to sacrifice Andromeda to the monster. Because his land faced destruction, Cepheus chained Andromeda to a rock by the sea shore and left her to be devoured. Luckily, the Greek hero Perseus arrived on his winged horse Bellerophon in Ethiopia just in time to fall in love with the beautiful young princess and attack the wicked sea monster as it approached her. After Perseus defeated it, the two were immediately married. Here one of Andromeda's attendants, wearing an elaborate gown, sits on the shore.

From a crater from Capua, 5th cent. B.C. Berlin, *Die Antikensammlungen*

Παραγενόμενος δὲ εἰς Αἰθιοπίαν, ἧς ἐβασίλευε Κηφεύς, εὗρε τὴν τούτου θυγατέρα Ἀνδρομέδαν παρακειμένην βορὰν θαλασσίῳ κήτει.

Apollodorus, *The Library* 2.4

A brush hanging on the wall reveals that the scene takes place in the horse's stall. The horse appears restless and the youth calms him, perhaps with a comb. From their many appearances in scenes of horse and chariot racing, we know that blacks were very often jockeys and chariot drivers. Ethiopians in antiquity were famous for their skills as horsemen and animal trainers.

Right: A black youth tries to tame a horse wearing a panther skin. This scene was perhaps originally part of a larger memorial for someone. In the art of ancient Egypt and Ethiopia, panther skins were a regular part of funerary art. The strength and speed of these animals was thought to be magical, and the wearing of a leopard skin was believed to give these special powers to its wearer. The same beliefs were held by the Greeks. The horse was also a powerful symbol that could represent someone's soul. The high quality of the craftsmanship and the beauty of this piece rank it among the very best sculptures to survive from the fourth century BC.

Left: from a kylix by Onesimos, 5th cent. B.C., Schimmel Col., Kings Point, NY, Here: from an Athenian marble relief, originally in colors; 3rd cent. B.C. Athens, National Museum

Homer, *Iliad* 4.143

κεῖται δ' ἐν θαλάμῳ, πόλεες τέ μιν ἠρήσαντο ἱππῆες φορέειν· βασιλῆι δὲ κεῖται ἄγαλμα,

From an Hellenistic bronze found off
Cape Artemisium, 2nd cent. B.C.
Athens, National Museum

Stories of the skill of blacks in training and working with animals are common. For example, the philosopher Seneca once related the story of an Ethiopian who trained elephants to fall to their knees and walk ropes at his command. The poet Martial even spoke of a black trainer who taught his elephants to dance. That must have been something to see! Here a youth rides his swift horse in a race. Winning jockeys had to be not only skilled, but also as light as possible—hence the young age of the rider.

Enlarged from an intaglio
on a gold ring, 5th cent. B.C.
Boston, Museum of Fine Arts

This portrait reminds us that some Ethiopian traders probably immigrated with their families to the Greek city-states. It is often forgotten that the Greeks were very much engaged in trade and commerce with people from all over.

οἱ δὲ Αἰθίοπες οὗτοι ἐς τοὺς ὁ Καμβύσης λέγονται εἶναι μέγιστοι καὶ κάλλιστοι ἀνθρώπων πάντων.

Herodotus III.20

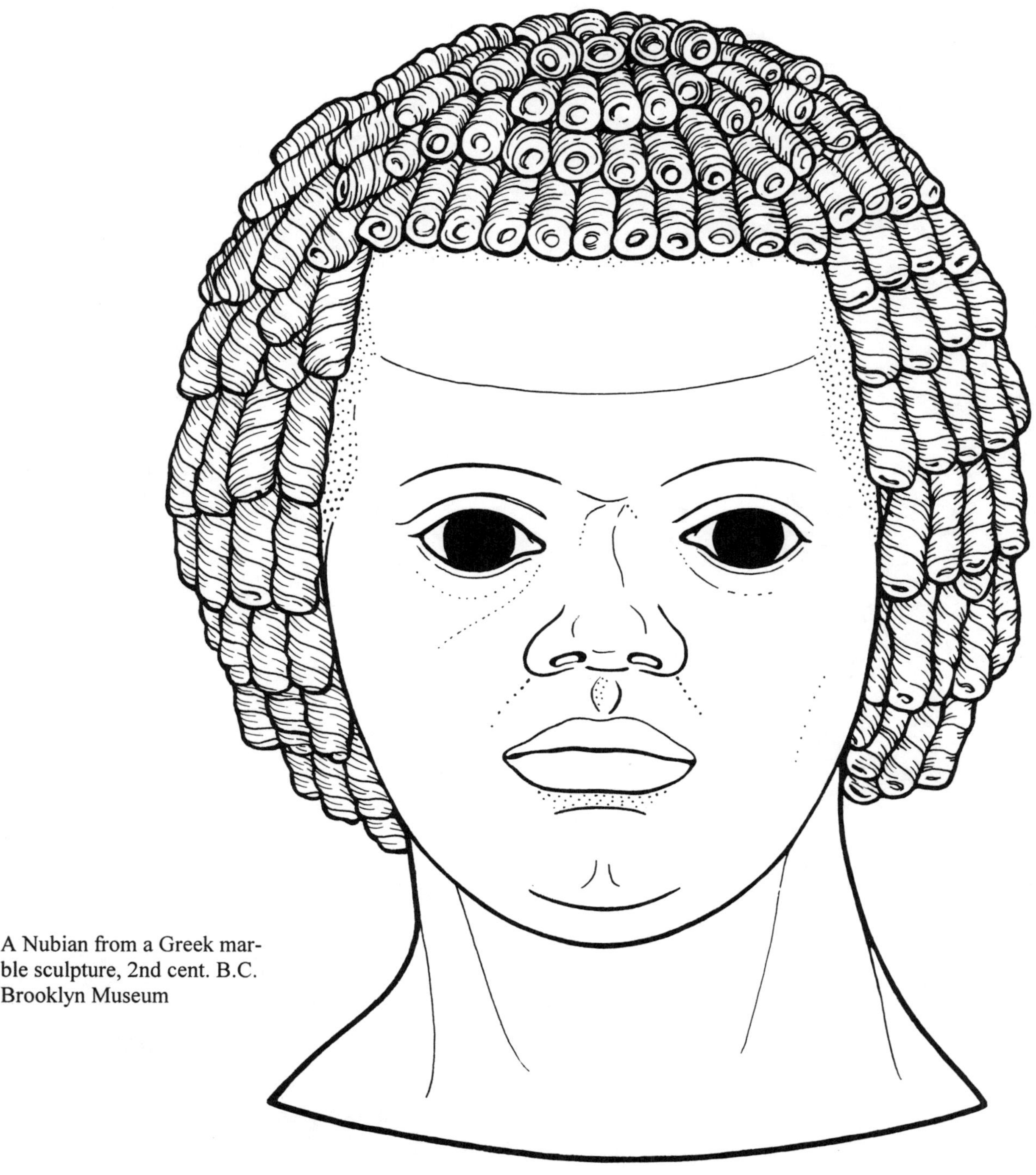

A Nubian from a Greek marble sculpture, 2nd cent. B.C. Brooklyn Museum

Few people in history have been more fascinated by and in love with the features of the human body than the Greeks. Herodotus, the fifth-century BC historian, reports that Ethiopians were reputed to be the tallest and the most beautiful people of all. The large number of portrait heads, sculpture, and other artwork showing blacks throughout antiquity seem to prove that this opinion was widely held by the Greeks.

Here an Ethiopian wearing Greek hoplite armor and a plumed helmet picks up his shield and looks at his sword hanging on the wall before him. On his shield is painted a griffon. The scene reminds us that black Africans sometimes fought as regular infantry soldiers alongside Greeks.

From a lekythos from Cumae,
Naples, *Museo Nazionale*

καὶ ἀντὶ μὲν λόφου ἡ λοφιὴ κατέχρα, τὰ δὲ ὦτα τῶν ἵππων ὀρθὰ περηγότα εἶχον· προβλήματα δὲ ἀντ' ἀσπίδων ἐποιεῦντο γεράνων δοράς.

Herodotus, VII.70.2

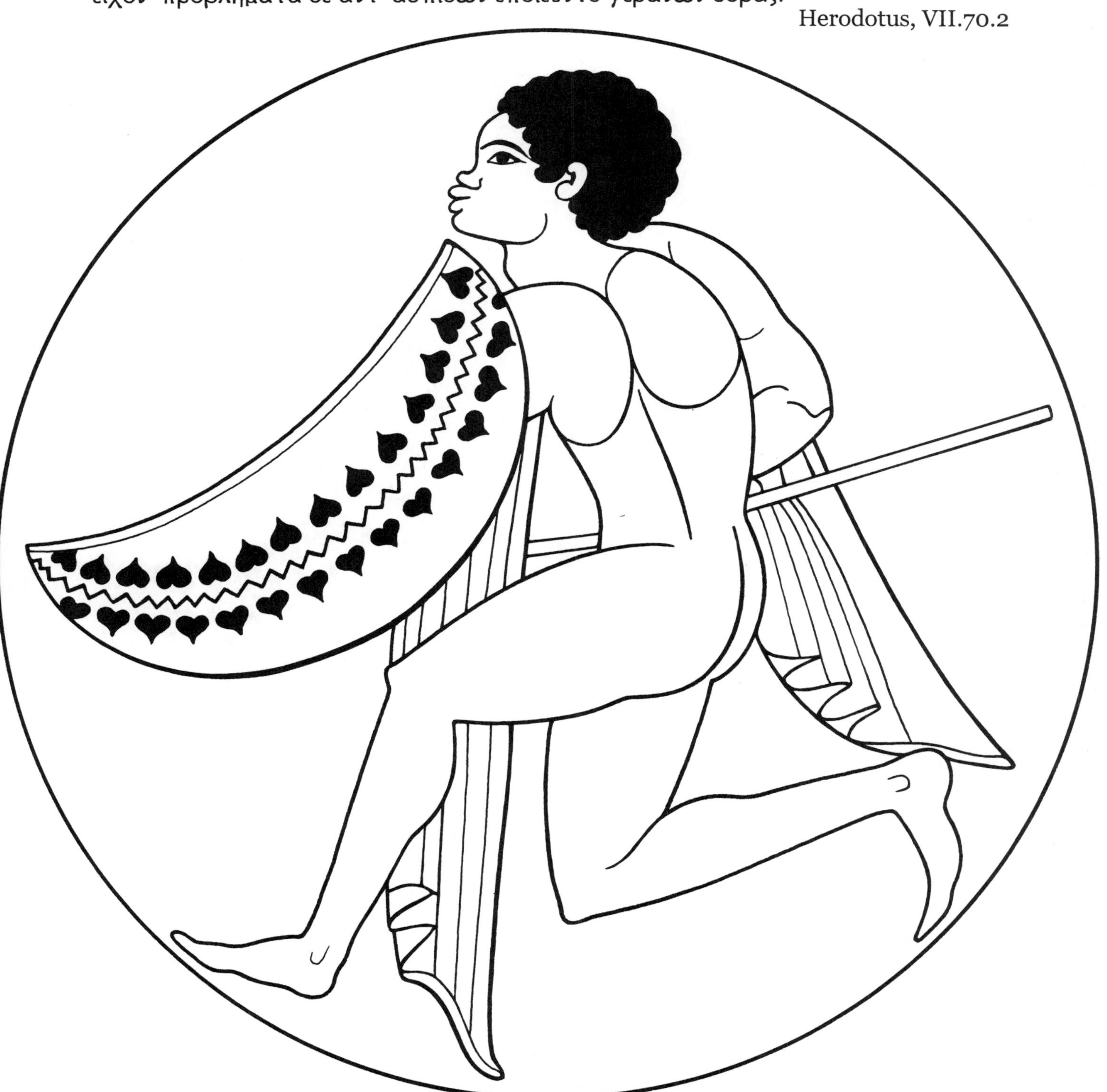

From the sixth-century B.C. on, Ethiopian warriors were employed as mercenaries in the army of the Persian Empire. An Ethiopian contingent took part in the battle of Marathon, when the Persian King Darius invaded Greece in 490 B.C. Ethiopian troops also took part in the invasion force of his son Xerxes, who attacked Greece in 480 B.C. Later in antiquity, blacks served in Greek armies, especially those of Ptolemaic Egypt, and in the Roman army. Here a young Ethiopian warrior, carrying a crescent-shaped shield and a spear, rushes swiftly into battle. According to the historian Herodotus, the shields of these warriors were made from the skins of cranes.

From a kylix, 6th cent. B.C. Paris, *Musée du Louvre*

"Homo sum: humani nil a me alienum puto." —Terence

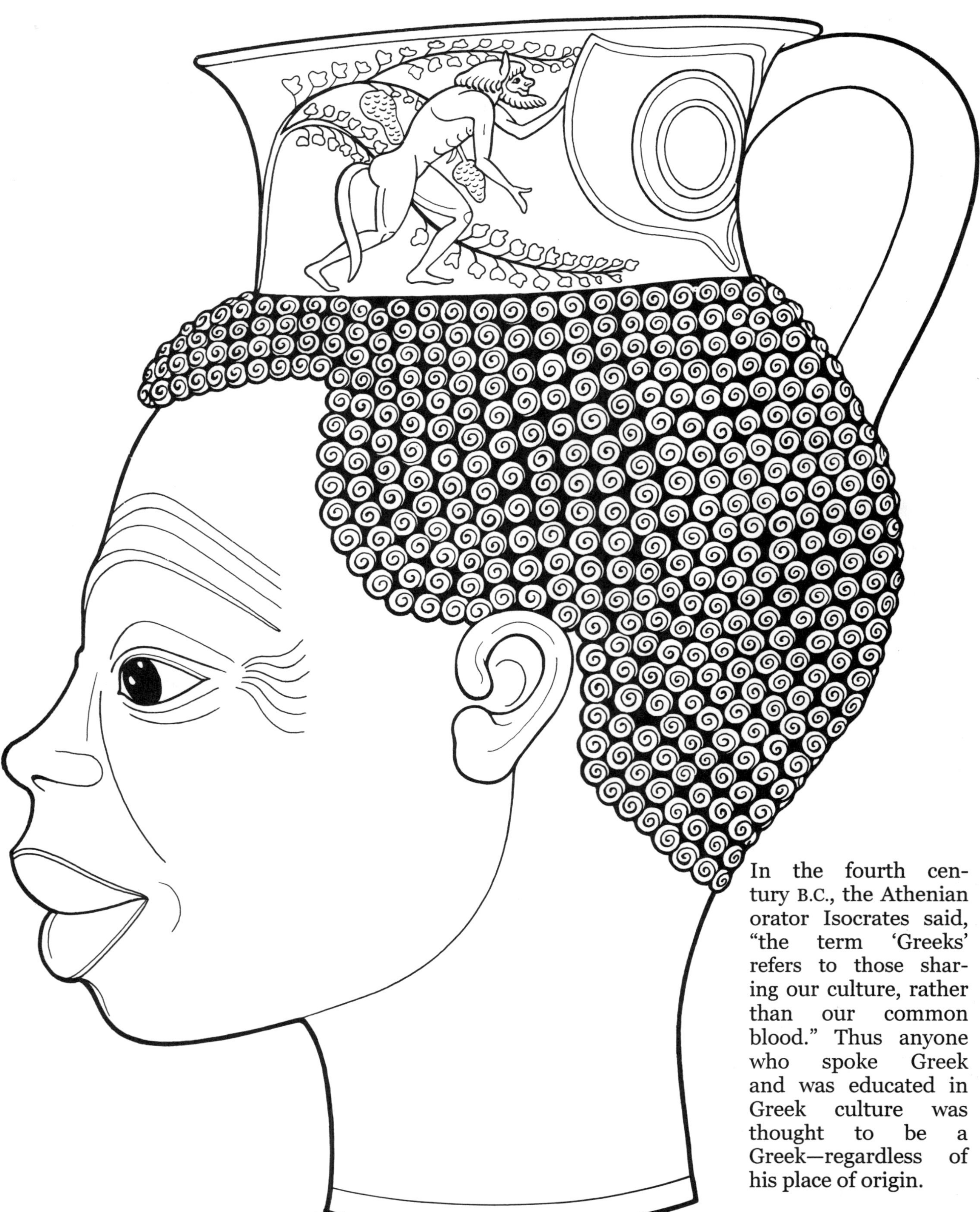

In the fourth century B.C., the Athenian orator Isocrates said, "the term 'Greeks' refers to those sharing our culture, rather than our common blood." Thus anyone who spoke Greek and was educated in Greek culture was thought to be a Greek—regardless of his place of origin.

Boston, Museum of Fine Arts